YOUTH

YOUTH

a collection of poems about growth

MASON QUIÑONES

Mason Quinones

Dedication

This collection is dedicated to necessary moments of heartbreak, naïve invincibility, irrational confidence, and self-doubt.

Foreword

Youth is ephemeral for the individual and immortal for the collective. Everyone must be young. Everyone must discover themselves over and over again. Everyone must listen to lessons of their elders and decide if those lessons resonate with truth or call out to be broken in favor of a new perspective. As such, we find ourselves enthralled by the concept of youth – mentally, physically, and spiritually. We are drawn to the concept and seek to emulate it, even as the body ages.

In our youth we feel invincible, incapable, enamored, empowered, scared and eventually resilient. In a collection of poems that chronicle my faltering steps over time, this book seeks to find patterns in the erratic experience of being young – things that make youth what it is.

> Consciousness
> Roots
> Yearning
> Curiosity
> Realizations

These central themes have been crucial to my understanding of my youth and my hope is that they resonate with yours. To fresh eyes; to uncertainty; to insatiability; to the emotions that make us feel alive...

to youth.

-MQ

I

Consciousness

youthful existence and confusion

Flying

I think I'm growing up today...
that must be what I'm feeling.
It's something awfully terrifying,
and at the same time oh so appealing.

I reflect about it incredulously.
I'm really not sure what has happened.
I feel like this airplane is taking off,
and my seatbelt is surely not fastened.

We're hurtling down the runway now;
I feel capable, empowered, and scared.
I might not know what the fuck I'm doing,
but in 20 seconds I'll be in the air.

Piecing this nonsense together now...
I think I've seen this bit in the movies.
It'll all work out how it's s'posed to right?
Isn't that part of the beauty?

Hurtling through the sky – we're flying
Look at me, I am the captain!
So many options clouding my mind,
trying to tune out all the distractions.

Figuring out how to guide my wings,
but it's nothing like what I've learned.
I went to drivers ed, no pilot school,
but there's no time for being concerned.

This thing with wings got an engine out back—
There's no telling where I might take it.
I might not know all the right details,
but let's see if we can make it a spaceship.

The sky's the limit for an airplane, I know,
but my ambitions don't only go that far.
I remember I don't know how to fly this thing
but I'll aim past the moon for the stars!

Woefully unprepared, but that's half the fun.
The speedometer just keeps going up!
Not sure what I'm doing, but I think that's the key
to this thing we call growing up.

Echoes

Onward, we dare;
to look back is to falter.
The unknown holds our prize;
the future is our altar.

At the feet of Courage we pray.
May she guide us true,
and to the face of Fear we say
I have no quarrel with you.

For we are in our prime,
reckless in our pursuits.
This is the life of the young.
We forge our own new routes.

The young are molten passion.
We are hot, burning bright.
When the world turns to pitch,
look to the young for a light.

Our power lies in reckless optimism,
an outrageous ideal for the future.
For if the world is broken now,
then her wounds we shall clean and suture.

Let us live with no remorse,
every mistake made a lesson.
Let us yell until we're hoarse,
the voice of life's great question.

"Why are we here?" we scream!
A jumbled echo our reply.
And so, we go on living,
the answer coming when we die.

Believer

I'm a believer
  In light
  In love
  In the power
    of our souls to heal

I'm a believer
  In darkness
  In hatred
  In the harsher realities
    we must consciously overcome

I'm a believer
  In free will
  In choices
  In the responsibility
    we have to build a better world

Maybe

It occurs that

maybe

I was built for this;

maybe

I am strong enough;

maybe

I will find the growth I seek;

maybe

I am ready.

Fresh Eyes

Inexperienced and naive.
They'll tell you:
"That's not how it works here."
"You'll learn before long."
"Follow the directions."
"Practice makes perfect."

And look, it's all great advice...
for somebody else.

Your inexperience is a new key.
Your naivety completes the combination.
Together use them to challenge norms,
breaking barriers without trepidation.

Time has yet to dull you.
You scare the powers that be.
Nothing makes them nervous
like fresh eyes and curiosity.

Rise

Rise.
Rise like the birds at first morning light
Rise.
Rise on swift winds coming in from at sea
Rise.
Rise to the beat of your wings taking flight
Rise.
Rise like the voices of lovers set free
Rise.
Rise like the sun on the East side of the Bay
Rise.
Rise, it is time to go and conquer today

Patience

Stay your course, young man.
A soothing song plays to me, as I sit here
waiting patiently for the right decision
to make itself clear.

I suppose that's part of the lesson.
Keep moving, focus on your desired progression, and
the right decision
will come from your work.

Still it seems so strange right now. Life
feels like it's moving so quick, and
I don't know how
I've suddenly felt okay with that.

Stay your course young man.
The thought rebounds in my mind, as I
sit in this bus driving slowly behind
other cars that are all carrying someone with
dreams.

I'm moving forward and I'll get there in time.
It feels like that patience thing is growing. As
I think about it,
my youthful optimism is showing; see,

I'm excited for what these years hold for my people.

Still

Nothing has changed.
I'm still the same me.
Struggling with the same things,
still waiting impatiently.

Nothing has changed.
I'm still the same me.
Still writing out my thoughts,
still growing daily.

Nothing has changed.
I'm still the same me.
Still praying for guidance,
still stubborn as can be.

Nothing has changed.
Still in over my head;
still over-committing;
still avoiding my bed.

Nothing has changed.
I'm starting to see;
it's all your perspective,
so choose carefully.

Nothing has changed,
while my future comes to be.
Everything is different,
but I'm still the same me.

Obscured

drifting,
obscured,
secured, but unhappy.
content,
yet the contents of my daydreams elude me,
as I make do with the makeshift
things I've empowered so they can use me

Use me.

Use me.

I'm begging you to use me.
I need to feel worthy, need to feel needed.
want to be looked to when it's time for a leader
have to be busy, to avoid what I'm feeling;
been looking left and right for someone to believe in
...me.

As I,

I find that, I,

am drifting,
obscured,
insecure, but proud

I want you to hear me call out, but I'm not tryna be too loud.

See, I'm in these new surroundings with friends and joy abound,

so what is it I'm searching for that, don't want to be found?

Is it peace of mind? Clarity? Or maybe just the sound?

The sound of what I ponder back, in my own internal discussion.

The sound of a distant voice I think,

or maybe just good percussion.

Or, maybe it's the wrong conclusion, to which that I'm rushing.

I suppose that only time will tell.

We all know hindsight's 20/20.

I just hope the grand distraction, isn't something of my own invention.

22 years down, at least double to go,

but, for my youth, I know I'm impure.

I'm content, but looking for better, and maybe that's why

I'm obscured.

upstairs neighbor

So many thoughts:
I'm trying to be perfect;
I'm trying to be patient;
I'm trying to feel worth it.

So many mistakes:
Never doing just reacting;
I smoke too much weed;
I haven't been quite as active.

So many thoughts:
I'm praying for growth;
I'm hoping I get better;
I know progress is slow.

So many ideas:
I just want you to listen;
I see a future that I love;
I want it to come to fruition.

So many thoughts:
I'm trying to stay calm;
I'm minding my own business;
I'm moving right along.

Living

At what age
does inspiration die?
On what page
do we begin a "normal" life?

When do we decide to move on
to the real world?
"Grow up"

When does being joyous
become naivety?
"The world doesn't work like that"

What is the cutoff
for ambient happiness?
"You're a hopeless romantic"

\Where do we drop off
our life-giving dreams?
"Let's look at your resume"

Why have we decided
making a living
is more important than living?

Tracing Steps

18 years old two months ago, and here I stand in the
parking lot of a small town high school getting ready to
say goodbye to people I've grown up with. Truth is,
I'm not even aware
of the steps I'm taking because
common core and extracurriculars never taught me
how to walk

20 years old 9 months ago, and I'm packing up my
apartment with three best friends that just graduated, but
I've got two years left. I'm leaving for 6 months and I know
where I'm going
but the path ahead is unclear because I'm running through
the trees looking for a forest

22 years old 5 months ago and I'm boarding a plane to my
new home with nothing but a suitcase, hangover, and an
injured heart but I'm going anyway
because you have to learn how to fly after you run. I'm up
in the skies looking for cloud 9 but we're moving so fast I
can't tell which one it is.

23 years old 3 months ago and I'm coming up on a year with this fog and these hills, as I'm starting to find out that cloud 9 might not be a cloud in the sky after all. I'm gaining altitude and perspective with time
and I think I've found what I've been searching for

I'll be 24 years old 9 months from now and I've come to find that it was never about walking, running, flying, or climbing to any one destination.
It's always been
and is always going to be

about the journey.

Permission

Let yourself feel.
Your fears are powerful.
Your love is stronger.
Your joy is contagious,
and the world is brighter when you live it in color.

Let yourself think.
Your worries are important.
Your plans lead to growth.
Your ideas lift up others,
and your legacy is born from your wildest dreams.

Let yourself breathe.
Your sighs are relieving.
Your sharp breaths are exciting.
Your shouts give encouragement,
and your self expression helps others find their voice.

Let yourself live.
Your impact is boundless.
Your experience is unique.
Your contribution is unmatched,
and your future is waiting.

Manifest

I want to be reckless.
I want to be exuberant.
I want to be powerful.
I want to feel
all my emotions
as I felt them,
purely, when
I was
younger and untainted.

I want to dream.
I want to hold on.
I want to get goosebumps.
I want to see
the world in the
rose tinted lenses I
traded out for
these
blue framed glasses.

I want to read aloud.
I want to laugh.
I want to sing proudly.
I want to cry out
and express myself,
without remorse,

as I did
before this life
made me doubt me.

I want to sleep.
I want to relax.
I want to breathe.
I want to take a break
and feel unpressured
by the march of time,
as I did
before productivity
changed me.

I want to love.
I want to cry.
I want to grow.
I want to live my life,
consciously,
as the captain
not some passenger
along for the ride.

I will it to be so.

And so it will be.

Just begun

Fallen in love with many places.
Still haven't settled on one.
For though I have lived,
my life is just begun.

I've written countless poems.
I intend to publish some.
For though I have lived,
my life is just begun.

I've made a living in the fog.
Still I intend to find the sun.
For though I have lived,
my life is just begun.

I chronicle my life and growth.
These chronicles are far from done.
For though I have lived,
my life is just begun.

2

Roots

things that knew you before you did

Seeds

There can be no doubt that the trees in a grove remember
their roots–
planted where their forebears once stood.
But, what of the seeds?
The wayward acorn,
the lonely pinecone,
flung far by the whims of the wind?

I cannot speak for all,
but I know one lone pod of a yucca, that found purchase
by the bay,
that now sits planted in the snow,

– remains resolute.
– remembers roots in the desert clay.

Clusters

I heard our souls have clusters,
that we grow like grapes on the vine,

connected to our people
from one life
to the next.

We come from the same soil.
We were nurtured by the same sun, rain, and air,
and though we may be picked at different times,
scattered through a dozen vintages and cellars,
our seeds go back in that common soil.
They are nurtured to sprout once more.
We find ourselves growing on the vine again,
with our cluster,
wondering how we ever got this lucky.

I heard our souls have clusters,
that we grow like grapes on the vine–
that the cycle of life will scatter us, and bring our cluster
together in due time.

I heard our souls have clusters,
that we grow like grapes on the vine;
and for all of the clusters in the vineyard, I'm grateful
that you're part of mine.

The Wanderer

In days of old
it was shown in scar.
The signs of a traveler –
one who had wandered far.

Scrapes from brush,
callouses on his feet,
sun-kissed skin,
hair far from neat.

As the ages passed by,
still onward he travelled.
New adventures came
as the future unraveled.

By foot or by horse,
then on to a carriage.
This love ensnared him
with a devotion like marriage.

To the journey he was wed,
vowing to wander and explore.
There was always a new corner –
always time for one more.

Still, the ages trod on,
giving way to new adventures.
Though the world was more known,
still he was indentured.

Each invention sped the process –
the automobile, airplane too.
Yet the infatuation never ceased.
He still searches for a view.

In days of old
it was shown in scar.
The signs of a traveler –
one who had wandered far

The man may look different.
He has worn many faces.
Now he has a carry-on,
a passport full of places.

The world is mapped and taught.
Mystery seems all but gone.
Still you can find him searching,
for adventure his heart has won.

Leaving

Do not miss me;
I have not left you.

My arms do not hold you,
but you will always be in my embrace.

My love is not bound to my body;
It will never leave you as long as you live.

I am on the desert horizon
where blue sky meets sunny gold.
I am in the kiss of the sun,
bringing warmth against the cold.
I am hidden in the peaceful night –
silent until you listen.
I am of the reflection on the waters,
smiling as I glisten.
I am the breeze that sweeps hair from your face.
Sometimes the one that musses it too.
I am in the smell of creosote and rain
washing down to engulf you.

I am in the mountains –
ever present as the stone.
I am with you all the way.
I think you've always known.

See, there's no way I could leave you.
I'm with you in rain or shine.
I'll always be in your heart,
and you'll always be in mine.

Places

I think that the clouds love the mountains, the same way that the fog loves the bay.

They linger so close in the morning before making their way off for the day.

I'm convinced they're both matches made in heaven, the signs left behind leave no doubt in my mind.

The fog leaves the bay green and mossy, and the clouds kiss the mountains with snow upon high.

It's the beauty of winter in both places, when the days are short, and nights are cold.

The mornings leave beautiful reminders of warm connections so many ages old.

Extrañándote

A veces te extraño,
y también a veces no;
de tus vistas y tus secretos,
volviéndome loco por tu amor.

En mi mente estoy a tu lado.
Somos conectados en corazón.
Te digo nada podría cambiarlo.
No te olvido, por ninguna razón.

Bebiendo tu cuerpo,
desde tu cabeza hasta tus pies.
Subiendo y bajando
siempre me quita del estrés.

Enamorado con tu soledad,
pero también me da dolor.
Sí gano a mi potencial,
no vuelvo vivir con tu color.

Cada mañana Dios te pinta
con rojos y naranjas maravillosos,
horas pasan, y al puesto del sol
no puedo creer mis ojos.

Las veces cuando te extraño
están más que cuando no,
pero cada vez me recuerdo,
siempre te llevo en mi corazón.

Home

Home is the desert heat warming me as I breathe
Clean air and the smell of chile roasting
Sunrise behind the Organs setting the day on fire
Clear skies and the sound of wind rustling the leaves of
a pecan orchard

Home is the smell of creosote when it rains
The lightning and thunder of a summer night monsoon
A stack of enchiladas with an egg on top
Sunset over the valley with painted skies and pink
mountains fading to purple

Home is two wagging tails
Coffee with Mama in the morning
Chile rojo, papas and eggs to start the day
and the lonely places where I became who I am

Mama

I often think back to the moments that we shared when I
was young,
or younger I suppose.
I know I'll always be your baby boy in your eyes.

I remember sitting on your lap while you read me Shel
Silverstein,
or Robert Frost as I got older,
but it was your poem on the wall that made me want to
try.

I remember walking along the ditch banks by the
orchards with wind stirring the leaves.
Cottonwoods sound sweeter you would say,
but your company was sweeter still if you ask me

I remember sleeping on the colchón in your room while
dad was gone.
You were both parents while he was away,
but if it was hard for you, you never let us see.

Ancestral Love

I remember cold mornings, dewy grass, and the rising of the sun. When troubles were far away and a mountain trail lay before me.

I can smell wildflowers and evergreen shrubs as we broke above the treeline, and I feel the wind that would carry the sounds of a creek where a friend waited for me with lunch.

In those moments, I took it for once in a lifetime. Yet, as I think back now, I realize that you are always with me, affirming that I will continue as those before did.

I feel the guiding love and wisdom sent towards this errant wandering soul, as I become cognizant of how far we've come together.

La Muerte

Death came to visit me, the other night I think
She came in, sat down and asked me what I'd take to drink
We talked and we debated, traded tales, and contemplated

my bad habits and
those of my family she's known before me.

We passed the night and as we ruminated, our conversation
  illuminated, the reasons we can't be together yet.

See I'm too young, and there's too much fun, in this odd life
  that I've yet to experience.

She's eons old, and her touch is far too cold, for the likes of
  me to enjoy tonight.

I assured her as I closed the door, that there'll come a day
  when I'll want more, but at present we're just not there.

Death came to visit me, dressed in black satin and mink.
She came in sat down and poured herself a drink
asked if she was desirable, or at least what did I think?
She looked beautiful daggers at me, and I could not blink

as we traded our intentions in a gaze.

She whisked out the door with a smile and wink
Left me to sip on her ice cold drink

And I knew then
as I know now
that her visits are part of old family tradition.

Moments

What mattered in the moment will matter
as long as you remember the moment itself.

The memories we have with one another
fade if we forget
to remind ourselves how wonderful that moment was,
how grateful we were when happened,
and how excited we were for the next time
when it ended.

That's why picking up where you left off
feels so good,
and why we describe our lifelong friends
by saying that every time we see each other it feels like
we never missed a beat.

It's because they remind us of those moments.
It's because they help us create new ones for the future.

Essence

If you could talk to yourself at 9 years old,
what would you say?

Would the child you were be happy?
Would the child you were be proud?
Would they look up to you because of who you are
 or just because you're taller now?

Would you apologize?
Would you muss their hair and tell them it'll all be okay?
Would they recognize who you both are
 or would they just see another grown-up?

Time passes
and all things in this world come to change
and then fade,
 all but the soul.

The soul grows and matures,
but its essence will only decay if you let it

Tis the Season

As you get older, you'll see
it's never really been about the holiday

It's about the mornings spent together
with nothing to do
It's about the food nobody makes as good as Mama
It's about the company that knows you
better than anyone
It's about the love that draws you in
and reminds you of how far you've come

It's about home and the people who make it special

Roadtrips

Cold mornings before the sun would rise
He would wake us up gently and carry us to the truck
We'd set down on the maroon upholstery of the backseat
    Fidget
    Fuss
    Fight
then get tired
and I'd wake up hours later with your head in my lap.

I complained then;

I miss it now;

I love you always.

3

Yearning

young love and heartbreak

Windows

Look here.
    No,
    I mean here.
    You look at me.
    I'll look at you, and we can, not just observe,
    but maybe see,
    because,
    I heard eyes
    are windows to the soul.

At first glance,
we probably won't notice much—just a color,
a shape, and the awkward darting as we avoid the
connection—but we'll try again,
because,
I heard eyes
are windows to the soul.

We'll look away,
spend time observing other things and other eyes,
but, the more familiar these pairs get, the more we'll
connect. And maybe we'll
start to know a bit more,
because,
I heard eyes
are windows to the soul.

You'll see the brown of the dirt I grew up playing in,
the dust of the desert I call home,
the dark and the light that make up my worldview,
and that's just the start,
because,
I heard eyes
are windows to the soul.

I'll look back.
While our eyes lock
and time flows slowly for a moment,
we'll trade stories without speaking, and maybe
we'll start to understand each other,
because,
I heard eyes
are windows to the soul.

Stargazing

As a child from a small town,
there's not always a lot to do.
So you look up to the stars,
and lay in wonder at the view.

Sometimes I'd find the night sky inspiring,
sometimes it made me feel undeserving.
I used to think of elaborate stories
and simple analogies for what I was observing.

Sometimes it was shapes and stories;
sometimes an ancient roadmap for ancient beings;
sometimes I wondered if they were holes in heaven's
floorboards that made up our earthly ceiling.

Stars have been a fixture of my life for many years.
They have a pull upon my heartstrings.
They can calm my deepest fears.

There came a time when I made the connection,
when in my mind's eye it was finally clear;
I don't always need to look up.
I've been given stars down here.

My stars fuel my imagination.
They lift my soul up high,
and it breathes life into my heart
when I look my stars in the eye.

I am meant to gaze at the stars,
to seek understanding and always adore.
It's beautiful knowing my stars are with me,
no matter how far or wide I explore.

As a child from a small town,
stargazing is just what I do.
So I really hope that you don't mind
that I've been gazing at you.

Fuerte

Gente vienen y también van.
Así es el curso de la vida.
Pero yo me voy amarte.

Fuerte, pa' que nunca me olvidas.

Untethered

Untethered hearts
Love and passion abound
When I felt so lost,
you helped me feel found;

I don't know what I did to deserve you.

Mind and body intertwined
Sharing freely all we are
If I could I'd hold on,
from you I would never be far;

I don't know why you think I'm worthy.

Poetically stricken and unbridled
You set my very being alight.
A love I didn't see coming
is the one keeping me up at night;

I don't know how to say this properly.

Heart's light in your eyes
They speak in eloquent ways.
Sweet words on your lips
that make me want to stay;

I'm at a loss for words.

Heart, mind and soul
You are simply divine.
If I had my way,
I would be yours, you would be mine;

I love you.

distance

I might not be next to you.
I might be oh so far away.
but my love is like the string tied between two cups.

Pull on it when you need to be heard, and I'll be there
listening on my end.

Complete

In the quiet morning hush,
as we lay softly in bed.
Your skin on mine gives me a rush;
in the space of a moment I am fed.
The air is still and smells like you.
The serenity befits your sweet mellow heart.
The birds chirping outside with sunrise
tell me that in a few hours we will part.

Your hair is cascading down your back,
over your shoulder, stray strands on your face.
A still frame of beauty lays in my arms,
and I know in my soul that this is my place.

You exhale softly and nestle closer;
I close my sleepy eyes and feel at home.
Early mornings with you in my arms:
The most complete moments I've ever known.

Sempiterno

It's in quiet eyes that linger, just a moment too long,
souls that together resonate so much it feels like song.

It's in the warm and gentle feeling of your head against
my chest,
a connection through ups and downs, synchronized
down to the breath.

It's in the way you listen, not just in the questions that
you ask:
a concern for present and future and a shared
acceptance of our pasts.

It's in your heart and soul, and the magnetic pull they
have on mine.
This triumphant feeling of love, the only thing that
conquers time.

Home

The sunlight danced in the corners of your eyes.
Your warmth drew me in as we mirrored the others
    smile and you hugged me close.
In that moment,

I was home.

The Cottage

Let's build something.
Don't tell anyone about it.
It'll be our little secret - a hideaway we run to.

We'll build it in the mountains.
Somewhere peaceful.
On our own,
surrounded by harmony.

It'll be so beautiful
Don't you see it?
There's nowhere I'd rather be;
oh, to hold you there.

So meet me there at midnight
We'll keep the pumpkin a carriage,
and the glass slippers will rest
by the door of the place we built.

When we're miles apart,
here you'll find me waiting:
open arms ready to receive you,
bursting at the seams to see your face.

Just make sure no one knows.
This place has to be our secret.
I'm trusting you with the idea.
I just hope we both can keep it.

It won't be like other homes,
It's just for you and I.
No neighbors and no guests.
No friends who can stop by.

It's a private place we've built.
You're all the company I need.
Why fuss over distractions,
you are all I want to read.

But, this place will be secluded.
Eventually you'll need more.
So then I'll have to wave goodbye to you
while I'm weeping in the door.

Cottages were made for getaways.
Ours in the mountains is perfect proof.
Fact is you need real stability, but
passionate intentions don't make a roof.

I'll visit our place from time to time...
maybe open the door and look around inside,
eventually look upon where I held you and sigh.
While my heart still beats, there'll be tears in my eyes.

We built something together - a place we knew we couldn't
stay.
We pushed past all the warnings.
We built it anyway.

I know you cannot stay any longer;
We cannot linger in our place,
but, as you cross the threshold,
know that I'll love you all my days.

trial & error

I swear to you that nothing can change the way I feel
about you, not in this life or the next.

See there's nothing quite like the way that your heart fits
to mine,
and there's no way another soul could ever intertwine
itself into my being the same way I find
that you are simply hard coded into my existence now.

I'm ashamed to tell you that's it's not because I didn't
try
to push your memory out of my
mind
in the healthiest manner that I could
find.

And, well,
it's just trying to heal didn't work–I won't
lie. So,

I,
tarnished growth with the unhealthy affections
of forced feigned connections
that will now simply feel,

hollow,

because they could never hope to dull the feeling of
having lost you.

Temporary

Be my Valentine.
Don't promise any more.
Spend the night with me,
and then walk out my door.

No strings attached...
No false pretenses...
Forget social constructs;
let's live through our senses.

I won't whisper sweet nothings...
You won't have to call back...
If we make nothing of something,
then just leave it at that.

Be my Valentine.
Don't leave clothes on my floor.
Lie to me that you're mine,
and for the night I'm yours.

Don't wonder about me.
I don't belong in your head.
I don't mean to be cynical,
but I refuse to be misread.

What you see is what you get.
I can promise nothing more.
So be my Valentine, darling,
and then walk right out my door.

the way

I couldn't
I–
I don't
I... I can't imagine adoring anyone else this much
if they'd hurt me like you did,
and I think that's the saddest way I've said I love you.

Unsaid

I miss you
"How have you been? It's so nice to catch up!"

"..."

I miss you
"That's so good to hear. I'm glad you're flourishing, and I hope you know I'm proud of you."

"........"

I miss you
"Me? I've been doing good, just keeping my head down, working, and trying to write a lot."

"......."

I miss you
"Work has been busy, but I like that better than being bored so it's nice"

I miss you

no reply

I miss you

Fleeting

"Tell me what you're thinking. What's running through
this beautiful head?"
I whisper softly in your ear while you lay on my chest,
and I run my fingers through
soft long hair.
A breeze at the window ruffles the curtains,
and spare rays of sunshine
dance across intertwined legs sticking out from under
the covers.
You pick your head up to look at me,
light strikes your hair as it softly falls to one side and you
start a coy response, "...

I blink and I'm alone,
chasing a memory that set me alight.

Lonely

I've been lonely.
It's really quite a feeling.
It's like being in a room
with glass walls, floor, and ceiling.

Around me life happens.
Inside is my domain.
I can see when it's nice out,
but it's foggy in the rain.

There are glass rooms like mine.
I see them all around me.
The people inside are kind.
We talk about what we see.

Each room has a view,
slightly different from any other.
If it weren't for our talks,
I'd just stare out and wonder.

I wonder if you'd wonder,
wonder like I do.
Wonder when there's other
wonderful things to do.

But, all this wondering
has taught me a thing or two.
Everyone has a glass room.
Everyone's as lonely as you.

Lonely isn't bad.
It's simply the human condition;
it's why we talk about our room -
our universal affliction.

Falling

I fell once upon a time
It was a wonderful feeling
Wind in my face
Soaring above all
Exhilarating
   Oh I fell

I fell once upon a time
It was a frightening feeling
Couldn't see
Out of control
Terrifying
   Oh I fell

I fell once upon a time
It became a dreadful experience
Scared of the ground
Waiting to break
Miserable
   Oh I fell

I fell once upon a time
Such a scarring experience
Broken down lifeless
In shambles
Shattered
   Oh I fell

Then one day it was different.

Falling was scary
Eyes were shut
I didn't want to see my own demise
I took a peek out
Turns out falling was flying
and now I'm at home in the skies.

Learning

trial and error
repeated failures
Lessons Learned
   and then we try to get better

give what you want
ask what you need
Lessons Learned
   and then we try to get better

stumbling and tripping
projecting and desiring
Lessons Learned
   and then we try to get better

broken and aching
rebuilding and reopening
Lessons Learned
   and we try to get better

pray for guidance
remember where it resides
Lessons Learned
    and we try to get better

follow good examples
realize it's subjective
Lessons Learned
    as we try to get better

at love.

Thinking

I've been thinking, lately, about how fleeting it all is:
about how people search their whole lives just to find
connections like this.

Thinking about how loving your people is the most
important thing you can do

I've been thinking.

I've been thinking maybe I should call you.

4

Curiosity

questions about why, how, when, and more

The Voice

Are you the voice inside your head?
I wonder to myself as I write.
Or, is there another collaborator
  who interprets our line of sight?

Is the mind in my skull my own,
or is it a collective space?
In this world am I in control,
  or should I just know my place?

If the mind works in tandem with soul,
then where does the hearts place lie?
If the powers are divided, not whole,
  then what do these questions imply?

Is there an internal revolution afoot,
some bloody Bastille day ahead?
Am I overthinking my own sovereignty
  over what all occurs in my head?

If I sound crazy please carry along, there's no need for
worries here.
If the voice inside you feels this way too, let's discuss
once the coast is clear.

Buzz

I wonder if it's the familiarity of reality or the possibilities
of our imagination that entice us?

Are we enamored by what might be?
Do we feel enthralled to our chosen path?
Do we yearn for control of our search for meaning?
Do we just want the answer?
Why is the grass greener on the other side?
Why do we have to experience it to know?

The thoughts and questions about existence
zoom
        across   my   mind
like spam emails when you forget to unsubscribe.

until suddenly,
a buzz in my pocket
reminds me I've got
too much reality that I'm behind on
to be worrying about how the whole thing works

Wonder

I wonder where my ceiling lies
Wonder what I can do to exceed it
Wonder if it's defined traditionally
Wonder if I'll live to see it

I wonder why I think so much
Wonder if that's how everyone feels
Wonder about my dreams at night
Wonder if they'll ever be real

I wonder how I've made it this far
Wonder if I've really grown at all
Wonder how much higher I'll climb
Wonder to what lows I will fall

I wonder who made the world we live in
Wonder if any one faith holds the key
Wonder if the creator looks back on their work
Wonder if they're proud of what they see

I wonder when the world will wake up
Wonder if we'll ever take care of our home
Wonder if I should settle in one place
Wonder if I should just always roam

I wonder what makes me wonder so much
Wonder if it's a good use of my time
Wonder how Momma is always right
When she says it'll all be just fine

How?

How
How have I fallen
Given in to this urge again
I try and I try.
I plead and I pray.
I somehow can't seem to just keep away.
Oh, how?
How have I fallen again?

How
How have I fallen
Lost my self control again
I was doing so well
I was making big strides
Yet here I am again broken on the inside.
Oh, how?
How have I fallen again?

How
How have I fallen
Missed my intention again
I change my habits
Moved my life
Somehow ended up back here in this strife.
Oh, how?
How have I fallen again?

What If?

What if death isn't silent after all?
What if we just can't hear her talking until she's
whispering in our ear?
Like a mother carrying a sleeping child in from the car,
soft murmurs that it's time to go now.

Good

Do the good die young?
Or, is the that the young die good?

   untainted by the life they've been denied

Cliffs Edge

Is it beautiful release,
or cowardly flight
to give in to death's ease
and relinquish earthly plight?

Our time in this world
is both long and fleeting
So is it poetic, or is it weak
to speed to deaths meeting?

How odd must I seem

I want success in this life.
I'm impatient on my ride.
Yet I contemplate death
and the nature of suicide.

Don't take this the wrong way,
I've no interest in dying,
but the thought intrigues me;
I wonder if it's like flying.

To be free of gravity,
of all earthly restraints.
To be a soul and just a soul
with no body to taint

Alas I resolve
to live out my days,
but death I fear not
because I'll meet her anyways.

Who knows?

How many people know you?
The real you?
The honest you?
How many people know you?
The vulnerable you?
The brave you?
How many people know you?
The broken you?
The hidden you?

How many people know you as an idea
instead of a person?

Vision

The future that you see,
is it beautiful?
Does it scare you?
Is it outlandish?
I hope so.

The future that you see,
is it different?
Does it inspire you?
Is it unreasonable?
I hope so.

The future that you see,
do you want it?
Do you dream of it?
Do you believe it?
I hope so.

The future that you see,
will you build it?
Will you nurture it?
Will you show me?
I hope so.

Everything

It all revolves
around life's central question.
The answer to everything flows from it.
Your problems fade.
Your purpose is resolved.
Your worries are quelled.
Your fears are dissolved.
Your joys are realized.
Your plans will evolve.
Your confidence grows.
Your insecurities are absolved.
Your dreams will become real.
Your hardest test has been solved.

It would seem such a question might be too long to recall.
Might have so many facets,
it's hardly one question at all.
Truth is, no matter your answer,
the question itself is quite small.
So what could be the query
around which all of life revolves?

Simply put,

what do you want?

Questions for the mirror

Think about your voice.
Not the one you talk to me with, but
the one that's reading this right now.

What's the tone you're using?
Is there emotion or inflection?
If you could put a face to the voice,
Do you think you'd see your reflection?

Think about your heart.
Not the one pumping blood right now, but
the one that makes impulse decisions and loves.

What does it desire tonight?
Is it happy or is there a yearning?
If you could take its temperature now,
would it be ice cold or would it be burning?

Think about your feet.
Not the ones bound by gravity to the earth, but
The ones that carry you in your dreams.

Where are they taking you?
Is it a rough trail or smoothly paved?
If you followed where those feet led you,
do you think that you would be saved?

Think about yourself
Not the one you think you are today, but
the one you are in your ideals of the future.

What do you do every day?
Is there a passion that you're chasing?
If you could talk to that you right now,
would the questions you ask be invasive?

I hope so.

That voice is yours.
and the more you speak up with it, it'll get clearer.

That heart is yours.
and the more you follow it, the happier you'll be.

Those feet are yours.
and the more you wander, the more beauty you'll see.

That you is you.
and when you find them, it'll be in the mirror.

5

Realizations

lessons and apparent truths learned thus far

Present

Sometimes the best thing you can do is be present.
Live where you are.
Give thanks for what you have.
Focus on what you can control.
Love your people.
Look up.
Breathe.
Let what is in progress transpire,
and deal with the future

when it happens.

Footprints

Grass may wave sweetly in the wind,
tall stalks wilting beneath your feet.
Dried leaves may protest the weight of your stride.
Packed snow may crunch, voicing its discontent with
each step.
Shifting sands may slow your ascent.
The way will surely be lonely,
but,

if you've set out to forge your own path,

both faltering footprints and steady strides
will pave the way for others following the same light.

Sometimes

Sometimes this shit hurts.
And there's not just one scenario in my head right now;
I'm just talking about life.

People say:
"It's a dog eat dog world."
"It's lonely at the top."
and
"You're the hunter or the hunted."
But really,
they're just excusing the way they lash out as ambition,
and it's all
because,
sometimes this shit hurts.

People say:
"Keep a tight circle."
"I move different."
and
"There's snakes in the grass."
But really,
they're just rationalizing staying closed off and
walled up,
and it's all
because,
sometimes this shit hurts.

People say:
"I'm doing good how are you?"
"Not too much, honestly."
and
"It's all good, no worries"
But really,
they're just putting on a brave face for themselves and
for you,
so that nobody
knows that,
sometimes this shit hurts.

I say:
"I'm just trying to stay patient."
"It's all a part of the process."
and
"That's just the season of life we're in."
But really,
I'm just trying to placate the fact that I'm not satisfied
with my growth as a man so far.

and, well,
sometimes that shit hurts.

Time

Time heals nothing.
You're giving strength to the illusion.
You've been told for years and years,
so I understand your confusion.

but

Time heals nothing.
Time is not a doctor.
Time is not medicine.
Time is not a suture.
Time is not a bandage.
Time does not nurse you,
nor ease,
nor attend,
nor least of all care.

No.

Time is a construct.
Time is a concept.
Time is a dimension.
Time is a measurement.
Time does nothing
other than exist.

pass.
come.
and most of all continue.

Time could never heal.
It would have to interact.
So what of all the things
that time healed in your past?

It wasn't time I promise;
what happened was a decision.
You chose to let pain fade.
You beat memory into submission.

With each of your open wounds,
it is you that must decide,
and if it's not worth the pain,
don't just pawn it off on time.

There are things worth hurting for in life.
Remember that as you make your conclusion.
Have you decided to leave it behind?

because...

Time heals nothing, it's an illusion.

Years

It's curious to me that the years we give significance, and
the ones that we don't, begin like any other.
   bright sun rises
   bright eyes open
   a bit of stretching and yawning to follow

   a call from mom,
   a cup of coffee,
   and a bit of thinking about today and tomorrow

So here I sit,
and here I sip,
writing a poem to commemorate another year.

It's curious to me that the years we give significance, and
the ones that we don't, begin like any other.
   time spent doing things we love
   dealing with realities we've chosen
   time spent remembering the memories we've made
   time spent daydreaming about those to come
   basking in the warmth of today
   and thinking about what we're building for tomorrow

Here's to the many to come.

Fear

Don't conquer your fears.
Meet them.
Make introductions.
Befriend them.
See what you can do for each other.

Fear doesn't need you to cower and grovel,
maybe it just needs to be recognized
and treated as a contributor along the way to your
success.

Success

Let's follow the directions
Success is up ahead I just know it
Stick to the plan
I brought water and snacks
We'll throw on a good road trip soundtrack
and
We'll get there in no time.

We hit our favorite breakfast spot before the on ramp,
made sure we hit the bathrooms on the way too
and
Now we're off on our way
All we need to do is follow the directions
to get to

Success

Following directions is easy when you know where you're
going.
Conversation flows easy and the traffic is light,
so it's smiles all around
and we daydream out loud about
the first things
each of us is doing when
we make it to

Success

Hours pass and start to feel like days
Before long I realize
We're low on gas
Not one snack left
and I'm not even sure
I like who's
In this car with me
But I just remember it'll
Be okay once I
make it to

Success

We talk about the directions
Realize we all want to go to different places
and somehow
we're confused
because
we all know
we have one destination
in mind:

Success

I look to change lanes
and
realize the highway is crowded.
There's cars limping along
People screaming at each other broke down on the side of
the road
because they all thought they
were closer to

Success

I see a little red
sports car with a lonely
driver
pushing the pace
steam
coming out from under
the hood
but my man over there in the
left lane
is still pumping the gas
because he knows
Just. One. More. Exit.
till

Success

We work our way over
To the exit
And pull up to a beat old
Gas station.
Run inside and I chat
up
the cashier about our
journey to

Success

He says he's been
before
So I ask how he liked it
What he did
and he tells me
He ought to ask
me the same thing
Because
here I am
packed in a car with
people I love

And we're not where we started now, are we?

Blank Pages

Staring down at blank pages, begging for me to write
some story, some emotion, something to set my
imagination alight.
Staring down at blank pages, feeling like I owe them an
explanation for why a mind this busy can't seem to find
some inspiration.
Staring down at blank pages, almost like I'm waiting
for them to blink,
to ask about my day, to pour me up my favorite drink.
Staring down at blank pages,
now it's starting to make sense.
I turned creativity into an objective and haven't felt
that present since.

Staring down at blank pages seeing more than I did before,
seeing plans, seeing opportunity, and seeing what
I'm looking for.
Staring down at blank pages,
thinking they won't be blank for long, but if they are,
then I'm experiencing,
and I love proving myself wrong.

Staring down at blank pages, wondering how empty paper
could be so giving.

I've got a life I plan to chronicle, and I'd better get to living.

Wrought

In time you will find that what matters endures–
that though friends grow older;
that though time moves faster;
that though nothing is as it was;

that all which is wrought with love remains.

Connections

I remember the feeling a year ago,
      as if it was yesterday.
On the cusp of an adventure,
my current life seemed far away.

There was nothing you could have told me,
not a single word of caution,
no warning I would have heeded,
such was the pride that I was lost in.

Of the challenges I've since met,
some have almost left me broken.
Yet without them the person I am
might truly never have awoken.

I've grown and much has changed,
but I'm the same soul at my core.
A little older, hopefully wiser,
still always reaching out for more.

With experience comes perspective;
our realities may all change,
but hold on to your people
because love remains the same.

I won't pretend I know what I'm doing,
and I don't know why we're here.
But, I do know that our connections
make the confusion a bit more clear

spreading our wings

The hands move slowly on the clock when I stare, but time keeps flying by somehow.

It's counterintuitive, feels like someone's been moving it, because the calendar flips pages without asking my permission.

Rivers and roads, I listened to it then, and thought of how those days would feel. These days are those now, and it seems that I've found that only runways take me to my people.

We're scattered apart, still always close in my heart. Lord knows that I miss each of you more than words can express.

We say I love you when we hang up, our next visit can't come soon enough, but just know that I'm with you all the time.

I really hope you don't mind, but if I've claimed you as one of mine it'll take a lot more than distance to change the way we're tied. See, souls don't really know about time zones.

Yours, truly and always—feel my love with you even though you can't see me.

Youth

Lately I've been thinking of the way it felt then and why
    certain moments can leave us enamored for years

I remember the way the light shone that day, painting
    the world in shadows except for the flowers I carried
I remember the sound of excited laughter and the feeling
    of an unshakable smile
I remember the smell of late spring, creosote washing
    over the valley like a wave
I remember the taste of tequila, smoke, and carefree
    existence on my lips
I remember the warmth of the desert sun kissing my skin
    like she'd missed me and I'd been away far too long.

And I hadn't even left yet
And yet I knew how much I'd miss it
And I didn't know yet
And yet I felt it would be different

And you hadn't even left yet
And yet I knew how much I'd miss it
And I still don't know now
And I hope it was the right decision

And I still think about that moment
And I still relive it from time to time
And it was raucous and serene
And it was unstable and unwavering
And it was pride and it was terror
And it was a storm and it was peaceful
And it was good
And it was youth.

CPSIA information can be obtained
at www.ICGtesting.com
Printed in the USA
LVHW030607100221
678886LV00006B/575

9 780578 795591